I0794422

A Ticket to...

LEVEL 2

/ck/e/
/u/

DECODABLES BY jump!

Teaching Tips

Red Level 2

This book focuses on the phonemes **/ck/e/u/**.

Before Reading

- Discuss the title. Ask readers what they think the book will be about.
- Sound out the words on page 3 together.

Read the Book

- Ask readers to use a finger to follow along with each word as it is read.
- Encourage readers to break down unfamiliar words into units of sound. Then, ask them to string the sounds together to create the words.
- Urge readers to point out when the focused phonics phonemes appear in the text.

After Reading

- Encourage children to reread the book independently or with a friend.
- Guide readers through the phonics exercises at the end of the book.

5357 Penn Avenue South
Minneapolis, MN 55419
www.jumplibrary.com

Decodables by Jump! are published by Jump! Library.

Library of Congress Cataloging-in-Publication Data is available at www.loc.gov or upon request from the publisher.

ISBN: 979-8-88524-709-2 (hardcover)
ISBN: 979-8-88524-710-8 (paperback)
ISBN: 979-8-88524-711-5 (ebook)

Photo Credits

Images are courtesy of Shutterstock.com. With thanks to Getty Images, Thinkstock Photo and iStockphoto. Cover – ViDi Studio, Golden Sikorka, Iakov Kalinin, Duda Vasilii, YummyBuum, Tartila. p4–5 – Syda Productions, Jaren Jai Wicklund. p6–7 – Tyler Olson, StockImageFactory.com. p8–9 – M-Production, JenJPayless. p10–11 – Monkey Business Images, motive56. p15 – Shutterstock.

Can you find these words in the book?

buckle

cup

get

ticket

It is a ticket.

A ticket to get on.

Get the ticket. Get the cup.

Pop pop pop. I can get it!

A ticket to go up. Buckle up!

We can get to the top.

It is a ticket to go.

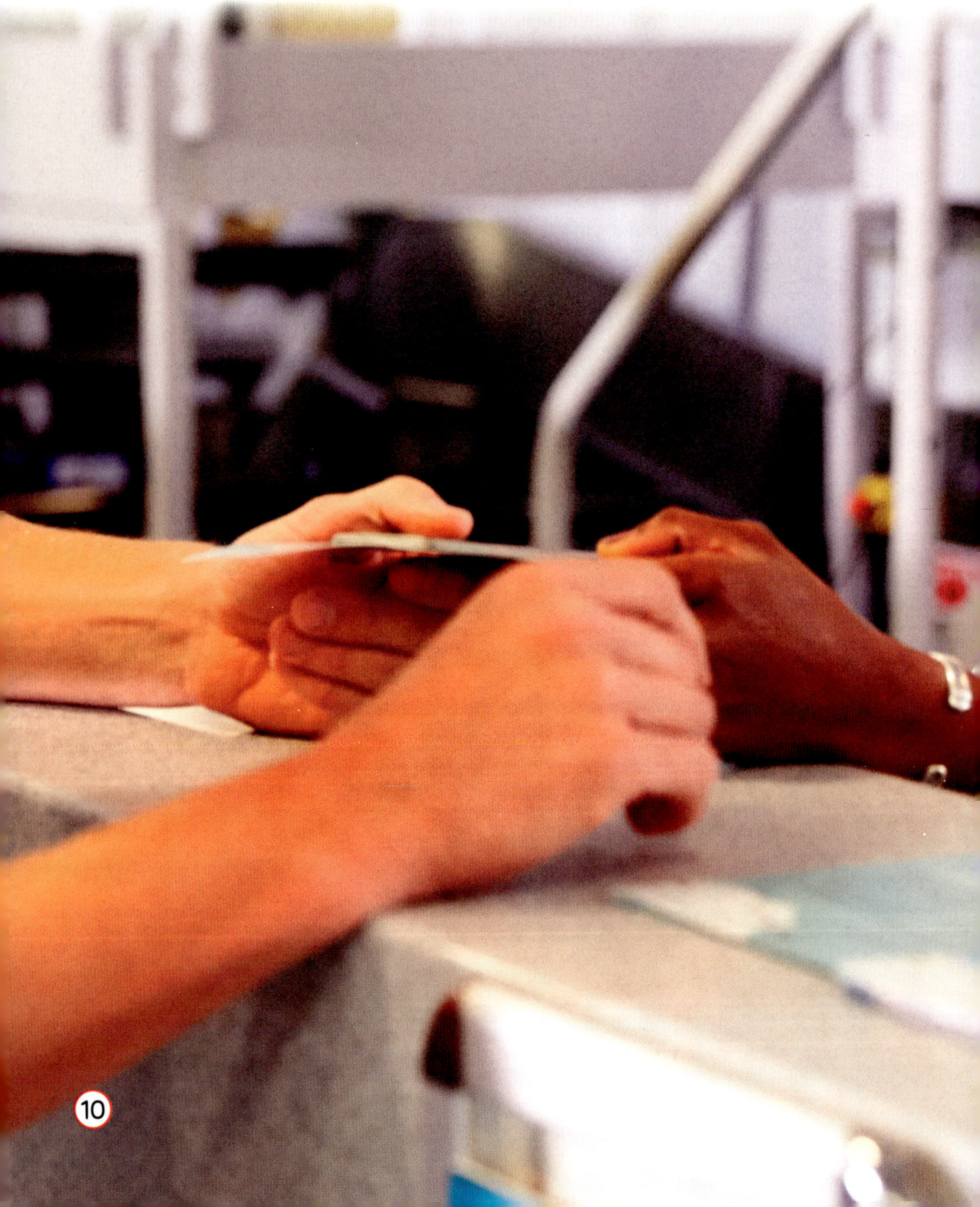

Up it can go! Up and up!

Can you say these sounds and draw them with your finger?

e

u

ck

Using the Letter Bank, trace the missing letter into each word.

buc__le

c__p

g__t

ti__ket

Letter Bank

k c u e

What other words do you know with the letters /ck/, /e/, or /u/?

tuck

bucket

locket

pocket

Practice reading the book again:

It is a ticket.

A ticket to get on.

Get the ticket. Get the cup.

Pop pop pop. I can get it!

A ticket to go up. Buckle up!

We can get to the top.

It is a ticket to go.

Up it can go! Up and up!